Rays Of Sunshine

Rays Of Sunshine

A 30-Day Devotional: Basking in the Sunshine
of Our Lord, Jesus Christ.

Christabel Bob Manuel

Rays Of Sunshine / Christabel Bob Manuel
ISBN: 979-8-8691-3803-3

Dedication

I would like to dedicate this book to my amazing children, Rex McIsaac Samuel, Divine T. Samuel, and Ivana I. Samuel. Throughout the toughest moments of my journey, their unwavering love, radiant smiles, and countless 'mummy, I love yous' have been my guiding stars, fueling my perseverance.

I would also like to express my sincere appreciation to Ada Monica Okoro, my friend turned sister, for standing firmly by me through the most challenging battles and providing unwavering support.

To my beloved mother, Professor Rosetta Bob-Manuel, and everyone who has uplifted and fortified me with their unwavering support, prayers, and kindness, I owe an immeasurable debt of gratitude. Your presence in my life has been an endless source of strength.

*Light is sweet, and it is pleasant for the eyes to see
the sun.*

— Ecclesiastes 11:7

Contents

Introduction

As someone who has counseled many people from different walks of life, I know firsthand the importance of having a little sunshine in our lives. No matter what you're going through right now, there are powerful and promising words in Genesis 1:3 that I want to share with you, "And God said, 'Let there be light,' and there was light."

That's the inspiration behind my book, 'Rays of Sunshine.' It's a daily guide designed to help you feel loved, comforted, and empowered to overcome any challenge life throws your way. It's not just about understanding the messages in the Bible; it's about bringing the light of hope, faith, and inspiration into your life every day for the next 30 days.

Think of it as a companion on your journey, lighting up your days like the early morning sun, surrounded by the love of a kind Father. Experts say it takes 30 days to form a habit, and this book is designed to do just that. It is there to be your partner in helping you overcome any challenge by breaking old patterns of negative thoughts of self-doubt and low self-esteem. It's here to make you feel better and guide you towards a happier life by teaching you about God's love and how to live well.

So, how about we start a new habit - a positive one - with the assistance of this guide? Let's use these Holy Spirit-inspired words as a guide to deepen our faith, casting light on every dark situation, circumstance, or thought, all the while knowing that God is always right by our side.

Embraced by God's Unstoppable Love

For God so loved the world that he gave his one and only Son, that whoever believes in him shall not perish but have eternal life.
— John 3:16

There are times in life when we all crave to feel valued and accepted. It's not uncommon to feel insignificant and alone when things don't go as planned. But during those tough moments, we can always turn to something special - the enduring love of God.

According to Genesis 1:27, we're created in the image of God, which highlights our significance to Him. John 3:16 spells out just how much God loves us by giving up His Son for us.

God's love is unmeasurable and is beyond our full comprehension. It doesn't matter what mess we're in or how rough life feels, God's love is unwavering and solid. He loves us not because we're perfect, but simply because we exist in this wonderful creation of His.

The story of the Prodigal Son in Luke 15:11-32 is a real-life example of this boundless love. The son messes up big time, blows his inheritance, and hits rock bottom. Feeling ashamed, he decides to head home, hoping to be taken in as a servant. But when his father sees him from a distance, he rushes to embrace him, celebrating his return with pure joy. The father doesn't care about the mistakes; he's just happy to have his son back.

When we're feeling lost or like we don't matter, we can find comfort in God's love. Even when the world makes us feel anything but special, God's love is a reminder that we mean the world to Him. His love goes beyond our mistakes; it's limitless.

Let's be grateful for this incredible love that holds us up and draws us closer. When we pray, let's thank God for loving us no matter what.

Let's Pray:

Dear Heavenly Father, in moments when I feel the need to be valued and accepted, I will turn to Your enduring love that surpasses all understanding. I am grateful for being created in Your image, a testament to my worth in Your eyes. Thank You for Your eternal love that exceeds all my faults and shortcomings. Thank You for the ultimate sacrifice of Your Son, which is a deep demonstration of Your great love for me. I am grateful for Your relentless love that endures through everything. In Jesus' name, Amen.

Day Two

Unshakable Faith

And when Daniel was lifted from the den, no wound was found on him, because he had trusted in his God.

— Daniel 6:23

Daniel's story in Chapter 6 is truly inspiring. It's a powerful example of unwavering faith and resilience in adversity. Despite facing pressure and opposition, Daniel remained committed to God's standards. His steadfastness teaches us an invaluable lesson about staying true to our beliefs, even in challenging situations.

When others try to lead us astray or push us to compromise our values, we must stand firm, just as Daniel did. His faithfulness in prayer didn't waver even when he faced the threat of persecution. That's the kind of faith that moves mountains and doesn't bend or break when faced with trials.

Daniel's security was rooted in his trust in God. He didn't seek personal gain or please people, but rather prioritized his relationship with God above all else. And in the same way, we must anchor our faith in God, knowing that He is our refuge and strength.

God's faithfulness to Daniel was evident when He intervened and rescued him from the lion's den, showcasing His miraculous power. This serves as a reminder that when we remain faithful to God, He stands by our side through every trial, silencing opposition and turning adversity into opportunities to reveal His glory.

Remember, God works all things together for the good of those who love Him. Even during challenges, He has a higher purpose for each one of us. So, let's anchor our faith in Him, knowing He is always with us, guiding us through every circumstance and using our situations to fulfill His more excellent plan.

Let's Pray:

Dear God, I am grateful for the inspiring story of Daniel, who remained steadfast in his faith and trust in you, even in the face of adversity. Help me to follow his example and stay committed to your standards, even when I am faced with challenges and opposition.

Strengthen my faith and anchor me in you, so that I may not be swayed by the opinions of others or tempted to compromise my values. I trust that you are always with me, guiding me through every circumstance and using my situations to fulfill your greater purpose.

Thank you for your faithfulness and love for me. In Jesus' name, Amen.

Day Three

Embracing a New Day with God's Love

Because of the Lord's great love, we are not consumed, for his compassions never fail. They are new every morning; great is your faithfulness.
— Lamentations 3:22-23

In the book of Lamentations 3:22-23, we're reminded of something amazing: "The LORD's love and mercy never end. His mercies begin fresh each morning." These words show us how faithful God is and how He gives us a brand-new start every day. His love, like the sunrise, brings hope and endless chances.

Every morning is a precious gift, a chance to start again with God. When life feels heavy, know that God cares for us without limits, and His love never changes. Let these words bring comfort as you begin your day.

In the Gospel of John, there's a beautiful story about Peter. Even though Peter denied knowing Jesus three times, after Jesus came back to life, He met Peter by a lake. Jesus asked Peter three times if he loved Him, and each time, Peter said yes. Then Jesus trusted Peter to take care of His followers.

Peter's story shows how God's love never gives up. Even when we make mistakes, God offers us a chance to start fresh. Just like He renewed Peter, God gives each of us a new beginning every day, a chance to feel His endless love and mercy.

When we let negative thoughts about our past mistakes, or even injustices done to us, play in our minds, it can often prevent us from experiencing the positivity and warmth of God's love. However, Lamentations 3:22-23 reminds us that every day, we are blessed with new grace and hope. Just as Jesus renewed Peter, God offers us a clean slate each day to start anew.

Hold onto this truth inside you: God's faithfulness isn't just an old story; it's real and alive today. Trust in His never-ending love, and let each sunrise remind you of His daily renewal and fresh mercy waiting for you.

Let's Pray:

Dear God, thank you for your never-ending love and mercy, which begin afresh each morning. Today, I come to you with a humble heart, ready to receive your grace and hope. Help me to let go of negative thoughts and past mistakes that prevent me from experiencing the positivity and warmth of your love. Please renew me today, just as you renewed Peter, and give me a clean slate to start anew. Help me to trust in your faithfulness and never-ending love, and to remember that every morning is a precious gift, a chance to start again with you. Thank you for the endless chances you give us, and for the hope and comfort that your love brings. May your love, like the sunrise, shine upon us and bring us closer to you. In Jesus' name, Amen.

Day Four

Guided by God's Word

Thy word is a lamp unto my feet, and a light unto my path.
— Psalm 119:105

Psalm 119:105 tells us that God's Word is like a lamp lighting our path. No matter where we are, it guides us. It encourages us to absorb its truths, brightening our present and leading us towards the wonderful future God has planned.

Think of God's Word as a light helping us in the dark—it shows us the way, giving us understanding and wisdom for our journey.

Life can be busy and overwhelming, making us feel lost. But God's Word brings hope and direction, ensuring we stay on track. When we read the Bible, we soak in its wisdom, understanding God's teachings that guide us through life's challenges.

In Exodus 3:1-15, Moses sees a burning bush untouched by fire. God speaks to him from the bush, telling him to lead the Israelites out of Egypt. The burning bush symbolizes God's presence and guidance, showing how God's Word can unexpectedly light our path, leading us to our purpose. Just as the burning bush guided Moses, God's Word is our guiding light, even in uncertain times.

Hold onto God's Word like a shining lamp. Let it brighten your life daily, guiding you through uncertainties and pointing the way to a fulfilling life. Just like a lamp brightens a room, God's Word brings light to our journey.

Let's Pray:

Dear God, I thank you for your Word, which is like a lamp lighting my path. No matter where I am, it guides me through life's journey, giving me wisdom and understanding for the challenges I face. I am grateful for the hope and direction it brings, ensuring that I stay on track even in uncertain times. Help me to hold onto your Word like a shining lamp, allowing it to brighten my life daily and lead me towards the wonderful future you have planned for me. Just as the burning bush symbolized your presence and guidance for Moses, may your Word be my guiding light, leading me to my purpose and fulfilling life. In Jesus' name, Amen.

Day Five

Firm Foundations

The LORD is my rock, and my fortress, and my deliverer; my God, my strength, in whom I will trust; my buckler, and the horn of my salvation, and my high tower.
— Psalm 18:2

Picture your life like a sturdy house. When we plant ourselves in God's Word, it's like laying a strong foundation, just as Jesus talked about in Matthew 7:24-25. He shared a story of two builders—one was smart, building on rock, and the other on sand. When storms hit, the house on rock stayed solid while the other one fell. That's how powerful a strong foundation in God's truths can be.

Psalm 18:2 paints a powerful picture: "The LORD is my rock, my fortress, and my deliverer; my God is my rock, in whom I take refuge, my shield and the horn of my salvation, my stronghold." Imagine God as our strong, safe place, our shield when life gets rough.

Remember David, the young shepherd who faced a giant named Goliath? Goliath was a giant, scary warrior, but David didn't back down. Armed with only faith in God and a slingshot, David stood tall. In 1 Samuel 17:45-47, David told Goliath, "You've got swords and spears, but I come in the name of the LORD Almighty." David trusted God's power, giving him the courage to face the giant.

David's story teaches us that even when odds are against us, trusting in God and His truths helps us defeat our own giants.

So, when life throws tough stuff our way, remember these stories and scriptures. They're like anchors, reminding us that sticking to God's truths isn't just smart—it's what keeps us steady and strong when life gets stormy. Just like a house built on rock, rooted in God, we can stand firm through it all.

Let's Pray:

Dear God, as I go through life's storms, I pray that I can be like a house built on a solid foundation of Your Word. Help me to trust in Your power and to have the courage to face my giants, like David did. I pray that Your truths will be my anchor, keeping me strong and steady through it all. Thank You for being my rock and my shield, and for always being there for me.

In Jesus' name, Amen.

Day Six

Think of This

The Lord is my portion, saith my soul; therefore,
will I hope in him.
— Lamentations 3:24

In Lamentations 3:21-24, the Bible says "But then I think about this, and I have hope: We are still alive because the LORD's faithful love never ends. Every morning he shows it in new ways! You are so very true and loyal! I say to myself, 'The LORD is my God, and I trust him.'"

In this Christian life, it's not just about understanding God's steadfast reliability or comprehending His boundless kindness. It's about going deeper about making these truths an integral part of our daily existence.

Take a moment each day to reflect on His un-wavering love and faithfulness. Revisit and meditate on these truths, for in doing so, hope will ignite anew, and your trust in Him will be fortified.

Consider this practice: every morning, give yourself a gentle reminder of the Lord's faithful-ness. Engage in a personal dialogue, a prayer that echoes with the blessings bestowed upon you through Christ Jesus.

Psalm 103 unfolds these blessings for us to acknowledge:

1. Your slate wiped clean? Your sins—all for-given.

2. Enjoying good health? He's also a healer.

3. Escaped danger? That's Him, rescuing your life.

4.   Feeling love? That's His unshakeable kindness.

5.   Life's little joys? He's the provider.

6.   Upholding justice? Especially in times of oppression.

7.   Feeling free? He ensured it.

8.   Wondering about His plans? He'll share them with you.

9.   Grace and mercy in challenges? That's His blessing.

Start each day by acknowledging these truths to the Lord. Whether through prayer or conversation, make these reminders a part of your routine. Watch as your faith grows, and you become more secure in His love.

Remember, my friend, just knowing about the Lord's blessings isn't enough. Speak of them each day—witness them become a vivid part of you.

Let's Pray:

Heavenly Father, I recall Your loving kindness to me. I recognize both Your significant and seemingly small blessings in my life every single day, and I'm grateful for Your unchanging and unfailing love for me. Thank You, Lord, in Jesus' Name. Amen.

Day Seven

Guided Through Uncertainty

And the Lord, he it is that doth go before thee; he will be with thee, he will not fail thee, neither forsake thee: fear not, neither be dismayed.
— Deuteronomy 31:8

When you find yourself in uncertain situations and you don't know what the future holds, take comfort in Deuteronomy 31:8: "The Lord himself goes before you and will be with you; he will never leave you nor forsake you. Do not be afraid; do not be discouraged." This verse reminds us that God's presence is always with us, and He will never abandon us. Romans 8:39 further confirms this: "neither height nor depth, nor anything else in all creation, will be able to separate us from the love of God that is in Christ Jesus our Lord."

Even in the toughest circumstances, we can find peace in knowing that God is with us. Psalm 23:4 reinforces this idea: "Even though I walk through the darkest valley, I will fear no evil, for you are with me; your rod and your staff, they comfort me." In our darkest moments, God's comforting presence surrounds us, providing us with the courage to persevere. While God never promised us a life without hardships, He assures us that He will always be with us, guiding us through the tough times and giving us hope for a better tomorrow.

Take Joseph's story in Genesis, for instance. Despite being betrayed, enslaved, and imprisoned, Joseph never lost faith in God. He faced numerous difficulties, but he never gave up on God. In the end, God used Joseph's struggles to help him become a leader and help others.

While I may not fully understand your journey, I want you to know that facing frightening challenges can be scary. However, Isaiah 41:10

reassures us: "So do not fear, for I am with you; do not be dismayed, for I am your God. I will strengthen you and help you; I will uphold you with my righteous right hand." This promise underscores God's constant support in challenging times.

Like Joseph, when life gets tough, remember that God is always there to help you. He promises to give you strength and help you through anything. Take heart, for you are never alone—God the Father, God the Son, God the Holy Spirit, and a host of angels stand by you.

Let's Pray:

Dear God, thank you for your promise to never leave me nor forsake me, and for your constant presence in my life. Help me to trust in you and remember that you are always with me, even when I can't see the way forward. Give me the courage to face my challenges with faith and hope, knowing that you will guide me through the tough times and bring me to a place of peace and joy. In your holy name I pray, Amen.

Day Eight

Encouragement for Every Day

In the day when I cried, thou answeredst me, and strengthenedst me with strength in my soul.
— Psalm 138:3

Psalm 138:3 reminds us that when we call out to God, He listens, making us bold and strengthening our souls. Each day, we encounter challenges that can weigh us down. It's easy to get lost in these problems, but we mustn't forget that God is right there beside us, ready to help us conquer those difficulties.

Sometimes, when we focus solely on our problems, we lose sight of God's presence. This can lead to discouragement and doubts about His love for us. But here's the truth: God is steadfast, always there to support us. When we feel overwhelmed, prayer becomes our lifeline. It's our direct line to God, who has promised to not only hear us but also respond with comfort and strength.

Consider the story of Esther in the Bible. She faced a seemingly insurmountable challenge—to save her people from destruction. Esther felt afraid and unsure, but she turned to prayer and found the courage to speak up. Through God's guidance and strength, she played a crucial role in saving her people.

The Bible is full of stories of people who faced great challenges and overcame them through faith and prayer. Philippians 4:6-7 urges us not to worry about anything but to pray and present our requests to God. It promises that God's peace, beyond understanding, will guard our hearts and minds. Also, Isaiah 41:10 assures us that God is with us, strengthening and upholding us with His righteous hand.

So, my friend, in those moments when life feels overwhelming, remember these stories and scriptures. They're like beacons of hope, reminding us to turn to God in prayer. He listens, comforts, and fills us with the courage and strength we need to face any challenge. Trust in Him, and you'll find unwavering support and encouragement.

Let's Pray:

Dear God, I come to you today with an open heart and a humble spirit. Please help me to trust in your steadfast love and to seek your guidance and strength in times of trouble. Give me the courage to face any challenge and the peace that surpasses all understanding. Thank you for always being there for me. In Jesus' name, Amen.

Day Nine

Endless Love

For I am persuaded, that neither death, nor life, nor angels, nor principalities, nor powers, nor things present, nor things to come, Nor height, nor depth, nor any other creature, shall be able to separate us from the love of God, which is in Christ Jesus our Lord.
— Romans 8:38-39

Psalm 31:7 talks about the joy that comes from God's unfailing love—a love that sees our troubles and cares for the anguish within our souls.

God's love isn't something recent; it reaches back before your birth and extends far beyond your days. It's a love that began before you even took your first breath and will keep going on, unending. God created you on purpose, seeking a deep and meaningful connection with you. That's why He's involved in every part of your life.

Think about the story of Moses in the Bible. Born during a time of adversity, his life started with the threat of destruction. Yet, God's love was evident even in those challenging circumstances. Moses was protected, nurtured, and guided by God's providence. Despite the difficulties, Moses became a key figure in leading God's people to freedom.

Let's include more scriptures. Romans 8:38-39 assures us that nothing can separate us from God's love—neither death nor life, nor anything in all creation. Jeremiah 29:11 promises God's plans for our well-being, giving us hope and a future.

So, when life becomes overwhelming, remind yourself: God's love is constant, reaching back to before time began and stretching far beyond. He deeply cares about every part of your life, understanding your struggles and pains. Trust that, like Moses, God's love guides and comforts, offering hope in all circumstances. You are embraced by a love that never falters.

Let's Pray:

Dear God, thank you for your unfailing love that endures forever. Help me to trust in your love, even in the moments when life feels overwhelming. I pray for your guidance and strength to face any challenge that may come my way. Please remind me that your love and care for me is steadfast and never-ending. In Jesus' name, I pray, Amen.

Day Ten

Incomparable Worth

I will praise thee; for I am fearfully and wonderfully made: marvellous are thy works; and that my soul knoweth right well.
— Psalm 139:14

Psalm 139:13-18 reminds us that God has intricately formed us, acknowledging His marvelous workmanship and His constant presence with us.

Have you ever wondered how to measure your worth? It's a question that often weighs heavy on our hearts. We can easily fall into the trap of comparing ourselves to others, believing that our value depends on our looks, possessions, achievements, or status. But this path only leads to feelings of inadequacy, envy, or even a prideful attitude.

A better way to gauge our worth is by God's measure. When we stand against His perfect holiness, we realize our own imperfections, and it's humbling. However, when we reach out to Him, something remarkable happens. His grace covers us, making us holy in His sight, though we don't deserve it. In God's eyes, each of us holds immeasurable value, deeply cherished, and loved.

It's important to remember that God doesn't compare us to others, and neither should we. Let's cherish His extraordinary grace, which knows no limits, and embrace the incomparable value that God sees in each of us. Through His boundless love, He transforms us, molding us into the people He created us to be.

Let's Pray:

Dear God, thank you for reminding me of my worth and for loving me unconditionally. Help me to focus on your measure of worth and not fall into the trap of comparison. Please transform me through your boundless love and make me the person you created me to be.

In Jesus' name, Amen.

Day Eleven

A Heart Aligned with God

Trust in the LORD with all your heart and lean not on your own understanding; in all your ways submit to him, and he will make your paths straight.
— Proverbs 3:5-6

As we navigate life's winding paths, we often long to live in harmony with the values that reflect the heart of our Maker. Proverbs 6:16-19 provides a clear blueprint, outlining traits that do not align with God's desires. These verses challenge us to examine our inner selves, urging us towards virtues that resonate deeply with His character. They are not restrictive rules, but guiding lights that lead us to understand God's aspirations for our existence. Let's explore these verses to adorn our lives with humility, truthfulness, kindness, and righteousness.

1. **Arrogant Glances:** God desires humility. Examine your mindset. Do you feel superior to others, or do you embody the humility shown by Jesus?

2. **Deceitful Mouth:** Trust is based on honesty. Aim for truth in every conversation. Lying weakens relationships and hinders spiritual growth.

3. **Hands Taking Away Innocent Lives:** Value the sacredness of life. Refrain from causing physical or emotional harm. Show kindness and love, recognizing the value of every life.

4. **Heart Plotting Bad Plans:** Watch your thoughts and intentions. Strive for a pure heart

based on love and righteousness. Let God's Word guide your dreams and goals.

5.   **Feet Zooming Towards Wickedness:** Be mindful of the paths you choose. Do not rush towards evil. Let God's truth guide your decisions.

6.   **A Dishonest Witness Spewing Falsehoods:** Value honesty. Avoid lies and let your words reflect God's truth. Be a testament to Christ's love and mercy.

7.   **Someone Sparking Trouble in Company:** Choose unity and peace. Avoid tearing others down; aim to uplift. Be a peacemaker, imitating the practices of the Prince of Peace.

These verses serve as a heart-check, urging us to adopt the virtues that matter to God. Let us seek His guidance and allow His love and wisdom to shape us into embodiments of affection, humility, and righteousness.

Let's Pray:

Heavenly Father, as Proverbs 6:16-19 reminds us, guide us to walk in the light of Your truth, avoiding detestable things. Grant us discernment to shun pride, deceit, violence, and discord. May our hearts be pure, and may our actions reflect the love and righteousness that You embody. In Jesus' name, Amen.

Day Twelve

God's Trustworthiness

It is better to trust in the LORD than to put confidence in man.
— Psalm 118:8

Have you ever found yourself struggling to trust someone, especially after being let down by those you once relied on? It's a common experience that many of us can relate to. But I want to remind you that God's trustworthiness far surpasses that of any human being. As Psalm 118:8 says, it's better to put our trust in the Lord than to rely solely on people.

What sets God's trustworthiness apart is that He isn't limited like we are. He remains faithful to His promises, no matter what circumstances we may face. People may disappoint us, but God stays steadfast and true. His track record speaks for itself—He has never once broken His word.

Let's consider the story of Abraham from the Bible. God promised him a son, but years went by without the promise being fulfilled. Despite doubts and uncertainties, God remained faithful to His word and ultimately fulfilled His promise, demonstrating His unwavering faithfulness.

In addition to Psalm 118:8, there are other scriptures that remind us of God's trustworthiness. Proverbs 3:5-6 encourages us to trust in the Lord with all our hearts and not rely solely on our own understanding. Hebrews 10:23 assures us that God who promised is faithful and doesn't change.

Knowing that God always keeps His word gives us unshakable confidence. Trusting in Him means relying on His unwavering faithfulness. Whether we're experiencing joy or trials, God's character remains consistent.

So, even though past experiences with people may make us hesitant to trust again, it's important to remember that God is different. His trustworthiness goes beyond human limitations, providing a solid foundation for our confidence. In God, we have an unwavering ally who will never fail us. His promises aren't empty—they carry the certainty and truth that bring assurance. Let's embrace the confidence that comes from trusting a God who has proven Himself time and again.

Let's Pray:

Dear God, I thank you for your unwavering faithfulness and trustworthiness. Help me to put my complete trust in you, and not rely solely on people. In times of doubt and uncertainty, remind me of your promises, and help me to rest in the confidence that comes from trusting in you. Thank you for being my unwavering ally who will never fail me.

In Jesus' name, Amen.

Day Thirteen

God, Our Unshakeable Fortress

But the LORD is my defense; and my God is the rock of my refuge.
— Psalm 94:22

During life's chaotic moments, it's important to remember that we have a steadfast protector in God, who defends us and shields us from harm. Psalm 94:22 (GNT) reminds us of this truth, "But the LORD defends me; my God protects me." It's comforting to know that God is our unwavering fortress, guarding us from every threat that comes our way.

Life can be challenging, and at times, it may seem like we're facing insurmountable obstacles, but we can take heart in the fact that God is a mighty protector. Just like a fortress stands strong against the assaults of enemies, God stands as our unshakeable stronghold. His strength is our shield, and His love is our security.

Psalm 18:2 (NLT) beautifully describes God's role in our lives, "The LORD is my rock, my fortress, and my savior; my God is my rock, in whom I find protection. He is my shield, the power that saves me, and my place of safety." God is not just a protector, but also our source of salvation.

In times of distress, we can find refuge in God's name, as Proverbs 18:10 (NIV) tells us, "The name of the LORD is a fortified tower; the righteous run to it and are safe." Imagine yourself running into the arms of God, finding safety and shelter in His unchanging character.

David and Goliath's story in 1 Samuel 17 is a great reminder of how unwavering trust in God's strength can lead to victory. David's faith in God made him triumph over his giant. Similarly, when we face our own giants, we must remember Philippians 4:13 (NIV), "I can do all this through him who gives me strength."

God's protection is not a one-time deal, but an ongoing promise. Nahum 1:7 (NIV) says, "The LORD is good, a refuge in times of trouble. He cares for those who trust in him." We can have confidence in God's goodness and take solace in Him being our refuge.

So, when life's storms come crashing in, remember to anchor yourself in the unshakeable fortress of God. His strength is your lifeline, and His love is your security. As you face each day, cling to the promise that God defends and protects you. You are not alone but surrounded by the impenetrable walls of His love.

Let's Pray:

Dear God, I come before you with a humble heart. I thank you for your unwavering love and protection, and for being my unshakeable fortress during life's storms. Please grant me the strength and wisdom to face any challenges that come my way and help me to trust in your goodness and faithfulness. Please guide me on the path that you have set out for me and help me to fulfill your will in my life. I pray that you continue to bless me and those around me, and I offer myself as a willing vessel for your work. In Jesus' name, I pray. Amen.

Day Fourteen

Our Unfailing Guide

Fear thou not; for I am with thee: be not dis-
mayed; for I am thy God: I will strengthen thee;
yea, I will help thee; yea, I will uphold thee with
the right hand of my righteousness.
— Isaiah 41:10

Have you ever considered, "Where could I go to escape from God's presence?" Psalm 139:7-10 gives us a glimpse into the enormity of God's omnipresence, reaching beyond what we can comprehend.

Imagine this: whether we soar high into the heavens or descend to the deepest depths, God is there. Even if we were to journey to the ends of the earth, from east to west, God is there, ready to lead and support us.

The psalmist paints a clear picture of God's unwavering closeness. It's like having a faithful companion, ever-present no matter where we wander. God's presence knows no limits – it's everywhere.

This passage beautifully reassures us in times of solitude and distress. It's a comforting truth that God isn't confined by physical or spiritual boundaries. He's with us, always, guiding and comforting us.

Let's consider the words of Isaiah 41:10 (NIV), "So do not fear, for I am with you; do not be dismayed, for I am your God. I will strengthen you and help you; I will uphold you with my righteous right hand." God's promise to be with us gives us courage in every situation.

I've found great comfort in meditating on God's omnipresence. Recall those times when you felt God's guidance and support. Let Psalm 139:7-10 resonate within you, reminding you of God's unwavering presence—a loving embrace that never fades.

Let's Pray:

Dear God, as I journey through life's twists and turns, I am comforted by the knowledge that you are always with me. Your presence is my refuge, and your guidance is my compass. When I feel lost or alone, I will remember Psalm 139:7-10 and know that you are there, ready to lead and support me. Thank you for your unwavering closeness, and for always being my faithful companion. In Jesus' name, I pray. Amen.

Day Fifteen

Finding Hope in the Depths

Save me, O God; for the waters are come in unto my soul. I sink in deep mire, where there is no standing: I am come into deep waters, where the floods overflow me.
— Psalms 69:1-2

The Lord promises that everything will work out for our good. Yet, sometimes, life's challenges make us feel like we're drowning, echoing the words of Psalms 69:1-2, "The floodwaters are up to my neck. Deeper and deeper I sink into the mire; I can't find a foothold."

Many of us have felt this way—overwhelmed by troubles that pull us deeper into despair. It's like struggling in quicksand, isn't it?

But here's the incredible part about the psalmist's plea for help. During chaos, he turns to God. He recognizes the need for divine intervention, a glimmer of hope amid the storm. Have you ever felt that connection?

This brings to mind the story of Elijah in 1 Kings 19. Elijah, in distress, found sanctuary in God's presence. Despite his trials, God provided comfort and guidance.

If you're struggling to find stable ground during life's turmoil, remember Deuteronomy 31:8. It's like grasping onto a lifeline. Surrender your struggles and find a firm foundation in God. He's an anchor—steadfast, unyielding, and unwavering amid life's tempests.

Life's challenges may seem like a sinking ship. But who can rescue you from the mire? Who remains an unwavering anchor even in the deepest depths? It's God—your faithful lifeguard in the depths, your unchanging rock in the shifting sands.

Remember, in the chaos, God stands resolute. His presence offers hope, His love gives strength, and His guidance leads us to solid ground.

Let's Pray:

Dear God, when life's challenges make me feel like I'm drowning, help me to remember that You are always there to offer comfort and guidance. Like the psalmist and Elijah, I turn to You for strength and hope during chaos. Please be my unwavering anchor in the deepest depths and help me to find solid ground in Your love and support. In Jesus' name, I pray. Amen.

Day Sixteen

Prioritizing Jesus in Life's Busyness

Come to me, all you who are weary and burdened, and I will give you rest. Take my yoke upon you and learn from me, for I am gentle and humble in heart, and you will find rest for your souls. For my yoke is easy and my burden is light.
— Matthew 11:28-30

A recent study highlights that people are busier than ever before, and often, they don't mind the busyness because they believe they're doing good – like Martha in the Bible. Life pulls us in numerous directions, engaging us in endless tasks and occasional worries. Yet, during this whirlwind, Jesus directs us to what truly matters, revealing the essence of being His follower, with Mary as an example.

Martha's heart is in the right place – active and dedicated, caught in the hustle. However, the worries of the world blur her focus. Now, let's shift our perspective: Mary simply sits with Jesus, hanging onto every word He speaks.

We each navigate our distinct paths in faith, and Jesus gently prompts us to prioritize His presence. Amid our everyday chaos, He whispers, encouraging us to pause and choose the treasure – the profound connection with Him that surpasses fleeting worries.

Practical Steps:

• **Take a Break:** In your busy day, create space for "you and God" time. Whether a brief prayer, reading a few verses, or simply being still with Him, it's crucial.

• **Release the Burdens:** Like Martha, we carry burdens. Entrust them to Jesus. Have faith that His presence brings a peace beyond understanding.

• **Choose Wisely:** Place time with God at the top of your priorities. Nurturing a close relationship with Him outweighs any task and brings fulfillment.

Remember, amid chaos, Jesus invites us to find rest in His presence. His companionship surpasses everything else. So, seize that moment, lean in, and experience His peace.

Let's Pray:

Heavenly Father, in the whirlwind of my days, I come to You seeking stillness. Help me carve moments for Your presence amidst life's busyness. Like Mary, may I cherish Your words and find solace in Your companionship. Take my burdens, Lord, and guide me to prioritize our relationship above all else. In Jesus' name, I pray. Amen.

57

guide me to prioritize our relationship above all else. In Jesus' name, I pray. Amen.

Day Seventeen

Eternal Hope in Unfaltering Love

May the God of hope fill you with all joy and peace as you trust in him, so that you may overflow with hope by the power of the Holy Spirit.
— Romans 15:13

In Lamentations, we find words that might seem heavy, yet within them shines a beacon of hope brighter than the darkest hour. The writer, often believed to be the prophet Jeremiah, shares a tale of despair and desolation. But amidst it all emerges a steadfast confidence, a lifeline in the stormiest seas.

The writer's bold declaration, "I dare to hope when I remember this," resonates as a battle cry. It's a reminder of unshakable hope anchored in understanding God's character. This courageous stand shows that even amid colossal challenges, hope endures. Why? Because God's unwavering love for us never falters!

God's love is like a constant lighthouse, unwavering amidst life's storms. It disregards our circumstances or actions, shining through our darkest moments. His love forms the bedrock of our confidence and hope.

"God's affection for us never fades! His compassion is boundless." Pause and absorb this truth. In a world of fleeting moments, God's love stands tall as an enduring torch. Each morning, He gifts us with a fresh wave of kindness, a daily dose of much-needed grace and care.

As we navigate life's hurdles, let's anchor our hope in God's unwavering love. When challenges loom large, remember each new day brings His unending compassion. Our hope isn't fleeting; it's grounded in the everlasting love of our Creator.

So, amidst life's storms, cling to hope. Remember, God's unwavering love for you is constant, His kindness always available. In this eternal hope, find courage, peace, and confidence, knowing you're embraced by an unchanging God.

Let's Pray:

Heavenly Father, in moments of deep pain and weariness, help me trust You. As I wait, remind me of Your unwavering faithfulness. Thank You for Your enduring compassion that never fails, regardless of the challenges I face. In Jesus' Mighty Name, Amen.

Day Eighteen

A Path to Fulfilled Living

Finally, brethren, whatsoever things are true, whatsoever things are honest, whatsoever things are just, whatsoever things are pure, whatsoever things are lovely, whatsoever things are of good report; if there be any virtue, and if there be any praise, think on these things.
— Philippians 4:8

In Philippians 4:8, Paul the Apostle encourages us to shape our thoughts deliberately amidst a world often crowded with chaos and negativity. Let's stroll through the timeless wisdom of these verses together.

Truthful Thoughts:

Begin by planting your thoughts in the fertile soil of truth—God's unwavering Word. Let His assurances be your steadfast guide, a beacon in times of doubt.

Noble Reflections:

Pause and ponder on actions marked by nobility and integrity. Seek honor in honesty, compassion, and selflessness, reflecting the character of our Lord.

Righteous Thoughts:

Dwell on what's fair and just. Let God's righteousness saturate your thoughts, influencing your daily interactions with justice and fairness.

Pure Contemplations:

Guard your heart against impurity. Choose thoughts as pure as a clean slate, untainted by the world's impurities. Let the purity of your thoughts echo the holiness of our Creator.

Beautiful Appreciation:

Marvel at life's charms, whether in nature, friendships, or acts of love. Embrace the beauty around you, adorned by God's craftsmanship.

Admirable Focus:

Direct your attention to the admirable. Celebrate goodness in others and let your thoughts gravitate toward Christ-like qualities.

Excellence in Mind:

Strive for excellence in all you do—in work, relationships, and personal growth. Aim high in dedication to God's purpose.

Praise-Worthy Reflections:

Lastly, dwell on things deserving of praise. Cultivate gratitude for life's blessings, recognizing God's goodness and faithfulness.

Aligning our thoughts with these virtues aligns us with God's plan for a fulfilling life.

Let's Pray:

Heavenly Father may our minds be sanctuaries of righteousness. May our thoughts reflect Your glory. Guide us to focus on what is true, honorable, right, pure, lovely, admirable, excellent, and praiseworthy. In Jesus' Mighty Name, Amen.

Day Nineteen

Harnessing Wisdom for Everyday Life

Wherefore, my beloved brethren, let every man be swift to hear, slow to speak, slow to wrath: For the wrath of man worketh not the righteousness of God.

— James 1:19-20

In James 1:19-20, we find a precious gem of wisdom that offers a refreshing pause amidst the rush of the world. James invites us to embrace qualities reminiscent of Christ—humility, patience, and self-control.

"Quick to listen" prompts us to be attentive, not only to others but also to the whispers of God amid life's busyness. It challenges us to nurture empathy and understanding within our hearts.

"Slow to speak" serves as a reminder of the weight our words carry. Proverbs 18:21 highlights the power of our tongue—it can bring life or death. As followers of Christ, our words should uplift, cheer, and reflect His love.

"Slow to become angry" gently encourages us to maintain composure. Getting angry often veers us away from the righteousness God desires. Instead, it invites us to display the peace and grace found in our connection with the Savior.

These verses aren't a rigid checklist but a call to live out Christ's life daily. As eager listeners, mindful speakers, and graceful responders, we showcase the transforming power of the Holy Spirit within us.

Let us allow the Lord to shape our lives through His Word, enabling us to embody James 1:19-20. May our lives overflow with His love and radiate His glory in every moment.

Let's Pray:

Heavenly Father, grant me strength to be attentive, measured in my words, and composed in my reactions. Help me reflect Your character each day. In Jesus' name, Amen.

Day Twenty

Embracing Strength Within

Ye are of God, little children, and have overcome them: because greater is he that is in you, than he that is in the world.
—1 John 4:4

"You, dear children, are from God and have overcome them, because the one who is in you is greater than the one who is in the world." Scripture: 1 John 4:4 (NIV)

As we journey in faith, challenges, and doubts often confront us, threatening our stability. The world may present hurdles that appear overwhelming, yet 1 John 4:4 assures us that as God's beloved, we possess a formidable Ally within.

God's Spirit resides in us, surpassing any opposition we encounter. In times of trouble, we find solace knowing that the One within us is greater than any force in the world. This truth transforms our outlook, granting us the strength to conquer.

This verse doesn't promise a life free of struggles, but it guarantees victory through Christ Jesus. When life brings challenges, let's recall that we're not alone. The power of God within us is our source of strength, wisdom, and bravery. Instead of relying solely on ourselves, we can access divine strength within.

Let's Pray:

Heavenly Father, thank You for the assurance that Your Spirit within us conquers every challenge.

Grant us wisdom to rely on Your strength, not ours. In moments of doubt, fill us with confidence in Your promises. Guide us to walk in the victory already secured through Christ. In His powerful name, Amen.

Day Twenty-One

Consistent Blessings from Above

Every good gift and every perfect gift is from above, and cometh down from the Father of lights, with whom is no variableness, neither shadow of turning.

— James 1:17

James 1:17 (ESV) tells us, "Every good and perfect gift is from above, coming down from the father of lights, who does not change like shifting shadows."

In this rollercoaster world, isn't it a relief to know that God's goodness stands firm like an unmovable rock? He's that "Father of lights," showering us with all things good. His kindness doesn't shift, unaffected by life's twists and turns. No matter what happens, our God keeps gifting us with perfect and wonderful things. That's the unwavering truth to hold onto when life dims our view.

The Bible is full of similar promises like Psalm 145:9 (ESV): "The Lord is good to everyone, showing mercy to all that He has made." Matthew 7:11 (ESV): "Think about it, even us flawed humans know how to give good things to our kids. Now, imagine how much more our Heavenly Father gives good things to those who ask Him!" And Lamentations 3:22-23 (ESV): "God's love? It never runs dry. His mercies? They're brand new every single morning. That's what I call faithfulness!"

As we ponder these verses, let's come to our Heavenly Father with gratitude and trust. His goodness isn't dependent on our situation; it springs from His unchanging love. In moments of joy, let's thank Him for His gifts, and in tough times, let's seek His guidance, finding strength in His unwavering nature.

Let's Pray:

Dear Heavenly Father, we're grateful for Your unwavering goodness. You are the Father of lights, the source of every good and perfect gift. Help us trust in Your unchanging love, especially in uncertain times. Guide us and strengthen us through Your steadfast nature. In Jesus' name, we pray. Amen.

Day Twenty-Two

Purified in God's Grace

Come now, and let us reason together, saith the Lord: though your sins be as scarlet, they shall be as white as snow; though they be red like crimson, they shall be as wool.
— Isaiah 1:18

In the divine courtroom of Isaiah 1:18, envision God as the Judge, not with a gavel of condemnation, but with outstretched arms of mercy. It's a scene where the focus isn't on judgment but on the restoration of brokenness. Here, God invites us, broken and stained by our shortcomings, into His presence. Instead of a stern legal process, He offers reconciliation, healing, and a chance to mend the relationship.

Our sins, likened to scarlet—a color symbolizing deep, enduring stains—are precisely what God addresses. He doesn't point fingers or demand self-imposed penance. Instead, His immense grace transforms these unwashable stains into a purity that mirrors the glistening white of newly fallen snow. This cleansing isn't about our efforts to scrub away the stains; it's about God's unbounded love, displayed through Jesus' sacrifice, that accomplishes this miraculous transformation. Psalm 51:7 uses the imagery of hyssop, a herb used for purification, to emphasize the depth and thoroughness of God's cleansing.

Reflect on the prodigal son—a tale of someone who wandered away, stained by regret and shame due to his choices. Upon his humble return, his father's overwhelming love and forgiveness were not withheld but lavished upon him. This story embodies God's heart towards us—ready to embrace, forgive, and celebrate the return of anyone seeking reconciliation, no matter how stained or broken they might feel.

Let's Pray:

Heavenly Father, as we come before You, we recognize the stains within us. Thank You for the sacrificial love of Jesus that washes us clean. May Your grace purify our hearts and lead us into Your radiant purity. Settle our troubled spirits in Your unending love. In Jesus' name, Amen.

Day Twenty-Three

Foothold

Neither give place to the devil.
— Ephesians 4:27

In the divine courtroom of Isaiah 1:18, In our Christian walk, it's crucial to guard our spiritual doors against the adversary. Ephesians 4:27 reminds us not to provide an opening for the devil in our lives. It's like ensuring our houses are locked tight against an uninvited guest who seeks to sow discord and confusion. The devil is cunning, always looking for even the smallest crevice to exploit and disrupt our peace.

We see a great example in the story of Joseph in Genesis 39. Despite facing various trials and temptations, Joseph maintained his integrity and refused to yield to Potiphar's wife's advances. He didn't give the devil a foothold in his life by choosing righteousness over temporary pleasures.

Here are some practical steps to secure our spiritual doors against the devil's advances:

Practice Forgiveness: Holding onto grudges or nurturing anger gives the enemy a direct invitation. Ephesians 4:26-27 urges us not to let anger linger but to release it. Forgiveness doesn't excuse behavior, but it frees us from its hold and safeguards our hearts.

"And when you stand praying, if you hold anything against anyone, forgive them, so that your Father in heaven may forgive you your sins." (Mark 11:25)

Guard Your Thoughts: Our minds are like gardens; they flourish what they're fed. Proverbs 4:23 advises us to guard our hearts diligently. 2

Corinthians 10:5 encourages us to take every thought captive and make it obedient to Christ.

"Finally, brothers and sisters, whatever is true, whatever is noble, whatever is right, whatever is pure, whatever is lovely, whatever is admirable—if anything is excellent or praiseworthy—think about such things." (Philippians 4:8)

Align Desires with God's Will: Our desires expose our true inclinations. Luke 6:45 highlights the importance of examining our desires, as they mirror our inner selves. James 1:14 cautions against being led astray by our desires, leading us into temptation.

"Delight yourself in the LORD, and He will give you the desires of your heart." (Psalm 37:4)

Remember, every decision, every thought either bars the devil's entry or opens the door wider. Let's be mindful of our choices and intentions, ensuring that our lives remain fortified against the wiles of the adversary.

Let's Pray:

Heavenly Father, grant us discernment to recognize the enemy's schemes. Strengthen us to resist his advances and guard our hearts and minds against his deceptions. May our lives be a reflection of Your truth and righteousness, guiding us away from temptations and closer to Your will. In Jesus' name, Amen.

Day Twenty-Four

Letting Him Mold Our Lives Like Clay

For I know the thoughts that I think toward you, saith the Lord, thoughts of peace, and not of evil, to give you an expected end.
— Jeremiah 29:11

Think about your life like building a house. Would you trust an amateur to make the plans or a professional architect? It's smarter to let an expert handle it, right? That's how we should treat our lives—letting God, the ultimate expert, guide us. As God's children, trusting His plans is crucial because He knows exactly what we need for a good life—things like strength, love, hope, care, and peace.

But how do we do that? First, realize that God isn't just a powerful being; He's also like a loving dad to us. He's in charge of everything He made, like Daniel 4:35 says.

Think of God as a potter and us as clay. When a potter works with clay, they have a plan—maybe to make a beautiful vase or a strong bowl. Similarly, God has special plans for each of us, as Jeremiah 29:11 tells us.

His plans for us are way better than anything we could come up with on our own. But are we like stiff rocks instead of soft clay? Our stubbornness is like that, resisting God's guidance.

If we ignore following Jesus' guidance, our lives might not turn out as great as they could. Without His help, we might miss the awesome future God has for us. So, it's smarter to let go of trying to control everything ourselves and instead, trust God's way. It's like letting the potter shape the clay—it's when we're flexible and trust His plans that our lives can be truly amazing.

Let's Pray:

Dear God, as the Master Architect of my life, I trust in Your ultimate expertise to shape me according to Your unique purpose. Help me to abandon my self-reliance and embrace Your wisdom, for without Your guidance, I risk missing the great destiny You have planned for me. In Jesus' name, Amen.

Day Twenty-Five

The Path to God's Holy Presence

Who shall ascend into the hill of the Lord? or who shall stand in his holy place? He that hath clean hands, and a pure heart; who hath not lifted up his soul unto vanity, nor sworn deceitfully. He shall receive the blessing from the Lord, and righteousness from the God of his salvation.
— Psalm 24:3-5

In Psalm 24:3-5, David, the Psalmist, asks a profound question - "Who may climb the mountain of the LORD? Who may stand in his holy place?" This question seeks to understand who can be close to God. The answer to this question lies in having clean hands and a pure heart. Our loving God wants us to be honest, let go of idols and be truthful.

To be close to God, we must ensure that our actions, like our hands, are clean. It's not just what we do, but the intention behind it that matters. Additionally, our hearts, where our feelings and desires reside, must be pure. True worship means surrendering ourselves completely to God, recognizing that He is the most important.

Idols are not only statues; they can be anything that hinders our relationship with God, preventing us from experiencing the Lord's blessings. We must introspect and eliminate anything that prevents us from being close to Him.

The psalm promises that those with clean hands and pure hearts will receive God's blessings. This is not just about material possessions; it's about having a strong connection with God. The ultimate prize is to have a close bond with

God, our Redeemer. As we strive to get closer to Him, let's aim for this incredible connection.

Let's Pray:

Dear God, cleanse our hands and hearts. Remove anything that stands in the way of us being close to You. Help us reject things that distract us and cling to the truth. As we draw closer to You, may we experience Your blessings and develop a great relationship with You, our Savior. In Jesus' name, Amen.

Day Twenty-Six

Embracing God's Forgiveness

If we confess our sins, he is faithful and just and will forgive us our sins and purify us from all un-righteousness.
—1 John 1:9

In our faith, forgiveness is a key component. When we admit our mistakes, God's faithfulness and fairness come into play, as assured by the apostle John in his first letter. He forgives us and cleanses us, guiding us to walk in His love.

Remember, when you make a mistake, Jesus Christ is always in your corner. Head straight to Him and accept His forgiveness. Let Him clean up your mess, no matter how big your mistakes are. He's always ready and eager to forgive and start anew.

Confession is not just admitting our wrongdoings; it's surrendering to God's transforming grace. By laying our faults before Him, we invite His cleansing power into our hearts. God's forgiveness is rooted in His unwavering love and Christ's redeeming work.

We often carry the weight of guilt, which can overshadow our spiritual journey. However, 1 John 1:9 urges us to let go of that burden through honest confession. Our Heavenly Father is ready to replace our guilt with His grace and our brokenness with healing.

Let's Pray:

Dear God, I come to You with an open heart seeking Your mercy. I confess my mistakes, knowing You're faithful and fair to forgive and cleanse.

Please wash away my wrongs and fill me with Your love. May Your forgiveness empower me to walk in Your truth. In Jesus' name, Amen.

Day Twenty-Seven

Boundary Lines

Your word is a lamp for my feet, a light on my path.
— Psalm 119:105

There are clear lines in sports that keep everything fair and focused, like staying in your lane during a race or keeping the ball inbounds during a game. These lines provide direction and safety, just like the guidelines God has given us in life.

Following these guidelines isn't about being restricted or trapped, but about finding our way to a fulfilling life. When we ignore them, we may experience consequences that come naturally from going against how God set up the world.

Consider Adam and Eve, who went against God's guidelines and ate the forbidden fruit. They thought it would bring freedom, but it only brought chaos and cut them off from the true blessings of life.

Instead of seeing God's guidelines as restrictions, let's view them as helpful signs that lead to a victorious life. By respecting His guidelines, we can experience the joy and fulfillment that come from living in His will.

Let's Pray:

Dear God, thank you for providing guidelines that keep us safe and on track. Help us trust in Your plan and follow Your path for our lives. In Jesus' name, Amen.

Day Twenty-Eight

Contentment in Christ

Let your conversation be without covetousness; and be content with such things as ye have: for he hath said, I will never leave thee, nor forsake thee.
— Hebrews 13:5

In a world that constantly tells us to do more, be more, and have more, it's easy to get caught up in the pursuit of money. But Hebrews 13:5 reminds us to steer clear of this distraction and instead focus on what truly lasts.

God promises us, "I will never leave you nor forsake you." This promise brings a sense of security and peace that surpasses all understanding.

No matter what uncertainties or financial struggles we face, we can find comfort in the unwavering presence of God.

True satisfaction and contentment are not found in material possessions or temporary pleasures, but in our relationship with God. When we align our hearts with His priorities, we discover a peace that cannot be found anywhere else. Money and possessions may provide temporary pleasure, but only a relationship with God can offer lasting joy.

Let's take a moment to reflect on whether we have been putting too much emphasis on wealth and material possessions in our lives. Let's choose to appreciate what we have and find contentment in God's presence. Instead of chasing after more, let's focus on our relationship with Him, knowing that His enduring love and companionship is the ultimate treasure.

Let's Pray:

Heavenly Father, thank You for Your promise to never leave us. Help us to find true contentment in Your presence and to resist the temptation to chase after material possessions. May we cherish the treasure of Your love and prioritize our relationship with You above all else. In Jesus' name, Amen.

Day Twenty-Nine

God's Timing is Perfect

For my thoughts are not your thoughts, neither are your ways my ways, saith the Lord. For as the heavens are higher than the earth, so are my ways higher than your ways, and my thoughts than your thoughts.
— Isaiah 55:8-9

God's timing can be compared to a clock that never rushes or lags, ticking precisely on time. However, waiting for things to happen can often feel like staring at the clock, endlessly waiting.

But here's the incredible thing about God's timing: it teaches us patience and deepens our faith. As we wait, we learn to trust in God's plan. And when tough times pass, we give all the credit to God.

Waiting for God's timing is like waiting for a meal at a restaurant. God delivers at the perfect time, just when we're truly hungry. He provides exactly when the time is right, rescuing us in His time.

It's essential to understand that God's timing is not the same as ours. Isaiah 55:8-9 reminds us that God's thoughts and ways are higher than ours. He sees the entire journey while we're only at the beginning.

Therefore, we must trust His direction completely, even when things seem bleak. God is not finished yet; He always adds a "but wait, there's more" to our stories.

Take Lazarus, for example. He was dead for days, and most people would have given up hope. But God added a "but wait" and brought Lazarus back to life.

The same goes for us! God can revive what feels lifeless within us, transforming us from mere survivors to champions.

Jesus' story is another example of how God's timing works. When Jesus died on the cross, it seemed like the end. But God had a different plan. Jesus rose from the dead and showed that even death doesn't have the final say.

Because of Jesus, death doesn't have power over us. He has the last word, and if we trust in Him, we become part of His ongoing story. Let's embrace the pauses in our lives, knowing that they are not endings but opportunities for God's perfect timing to unfold.

Let's Pray:

Dear God, help us align with Your perfect timing. We trust that You have the final say in our lives and that You will provide exactly what we need at the right time. May we find patience and faith as we wait for You to work in our lives. In Jesus' mighty name, Amen.

Day Thirty

Count it All Joy

My brethren, count it all joy when ye fall into divers temptations, Knowing this, that the trying of your faith worketh patience.
— James 1:2

God's timing can be compared to a clock that Many of us dread problems because they can cause us pain, confusion, and frustration. Life would be so much better without them, but the truth is that problems are a part of life. Inequality, sickness, and other challenges are all around us, and we can't avoid them.

However, James 1:2 tells us to "count it all joy when you fall into various trials." This may sound strange, but there's a reason for it. Problems are not meant to crush us; they are meant to shape us. They help us grow, build resilience, and deepen our wisdom. They can also bring us closer to God for guidance and strength.

Rather than seeing problems as something to dread, we should embrace a positive attitude towards them. Our goal should be to find joy amid trials, knowing that they can lead to personal and spiritual growth.

When God allows us to face trials, it's not to weigh us down, but to refine us and shape us into better people. We should seek His guidance, live by His words, and allow these trials to strengthen us.

Remember, tough times are not forever. This world is not our final home. There is something far better waiting for us – a life without pain or suffering, filled with pure joy.

2 Corinthians 4:17 reminds us that our momentary troubles are preparing us for an eternal glory beyond comparison.

Let's Pray:

Dear God, as we face trials in life, help us to find joy during them. Guide us to learn and grow stronger in faith, trusting in Your plan for our lives. May we have the courage to face our problems with a positive attitude, knowing that they can lead to personal and spiritual growth. In Jesus' name, Amen.

Biography

Christabel Bob Manuel hails from Rivers State, Nigeria, where her deep-rooted love for Jesus Christ blossomed during her early years. Her sincere devotion led her to become a dedicated Minister of the Gospel and a cherished Sunday school teacher, guiding others in their spiritual journeys. As a counselor, she offered invaluable support and guidance to those in need.

Presently, Christabel serves as the esteemed lead Pastor at God's Grace and Love Ministries in Cyprus, Europe, where she continues to spread the message of faith, hope, and love.

Beyond her spiritual calling, Christabel is a proud mother nurturing three wonderful children. Her passion for writing culminated in the publication of her debut book, "Rays of Sunshine," a testament to her insightful perspectives and inspirational words. Her dedication to her family and ministry reflects her unwavering commitment to enriching lives through faith and literature.